Contents

Introduction

A surgical mask or operating mask is meant to be used by emergency personnel during surgery and other emergency operations to remove microorganisms from their mouths and nose into liquid droplets and aerosols. The French physician Paul Berger used it for the first time in 1897 during an operation in Paris. Traditional operating masks are made of paper or other non-woven material and should be discarded after each use.

A surgical mask should not be confused with and approved to be a respirator. Surgical masks are not designed to shield the wearer from inhaling infectious bacteria or viral parts and are less effective than respirators for this purpose.
Face masks are one method used to deter disease transmission. Dental masks, safety, laser, medical, treatment and surgical masks can all be referred to. Face masks are loose-fitting masks, shielding the nose and lips, which have earrings or braces at the back of the ears. There are several different brands, and the colors are distinctive. It is necessary to use an FDA-approved facial mask.

Facemasks tend to reduce germ dissemination. If someone speaks, coughs or sneezes, little drops will come into the air and will allow someone to get sick. When anyone has facial masks, they can decrease the number of germs released by the wearer and prevent others from getting sick. A facial mask also prevents the nose and mouth of the wearer from splashing or body fluid sprays.

Health care workers

Easy surgical masks protect wearers against body fluid sprinklers in the mouth and prevent the transfer of body fluids from the wearer to others, e.g., the patient. This also warns users not to cover their mouth or nose, which, after a contaminated surface (fomite), may spread viruses and bacteria. These will also decrease the spread of contagious fluid gout (carrying bacteria or viruses) produced through cough or sneezing of the wearer. There is no convincing indication that interchangeable face masks used by members of the surgical team would reduce the risk of injury infections following clean surgery.

Research continues to minimize the risk of infections between many health professionals and in the population through the use of surgical masks. In group settings, facemasks need to be combined with other steps such as avoiding physical contact and ensuring good hand hygiene in order to minimize the risk of influenza in the United States Centers for Disease Control and Prevention (CDC).
For healthcare staff, safety recommendations prescribe the use of a facial-fit validated respiratory mask in the vicinity of patients with pandemic cases of flu in compliance with US standard NIOSH N95 or European standard EN 149 FFP3, to reduce the wearer's chance of potentially contagious aerosols and liquid

droplets in the skin. The CDC offers details on the goods of the manufacturers and the value of proper mounting of these masks (breathers). A printable information sheet was developed to solve rare respiratory problems.

General public

Surgical masks are commonly used by the general population in the countries of East Asia in order to minimize the incidence of infectious diseases. Throughout Japan and Taiwan, these masks are widely used during the influenza season to demonstrate concern for others and social responsibility. Surgical masks protect against disease transmission, and makeshift masks cover about half the number. During the pandemic in 2020, certain countries like Slovakia adopted mandatory masks in public transport and public spaces.

Surgical masks can also be used to conceal identification. Banks, convenience stores etc. in the United States have consistently banned their use as a product of offenders. During the demonstrations of 2019-20 in Hong Kong, some demonstrators used surgical masks to prevent detection, and the government sought to prohibit this use.

Design

Typical 3-fold surgical masks (Note that the top is right up and the bottom is upside down) The double-stitched border has been designed to cover the nose, and a metal cord is concealed inside to connect the mask to the nasal bridge tightly.

Depending on the style, the configuration of the surgical masks, the masks are normally three-fold (three layers). This three-ply material consists of a melt-blown material between non-woven textiles. The melted material serves as the barrier that stops bacteria from entering or leaving the mask. Most operational masks have folds or folds. Three plates are used to stretch the mask from the nose to the mouth. The mask is extended. Three different ways to secure masks are available. The most famous is the ear loop, which connects a string-like material to the mask behind your ears. The other is the tie-on composed of four unwoven ties tied behind the back. The sixth is the necklace, an elastic strap placed behind the back.

Surgical masks with decorative designs are common in widely used countries.

DIFFERENT TYPES OF MASKS

If you intend to wear a mask to prevent yourself from contamination, two styles should be identified.

Surgical face masks

Surgical facial masks are very poorly fitting, removable masks approved as medical equipment by the Food and Drug Administration. Doctors, dentists and nurses also wear them during their care of patients.

Those masks prohibit large droplets from escaping through the nose and mouth of body fluids that may contain viruses and other germs. They even shield people from splashes and sprays, including sneezes and coughs. However, the typical masks which you can purchase from a local pharmacy are not adequate to flush out viruses.

Experts are also suggesting special masks with a fine mesh capable of catching very tiny creatures. This must always be appropriately dressed for them to function.
The masks placed on the face will also prevent infectious viral spores, from cough or sneezing, from touching the eyes.

Respirators

Respirators are also used to protect the wearer from harmful contaminants of blood, such as bacteria, and are also used as N95 respirator masks. They are accredited by the CDC and the National Institute for Security and Health at work.

This is known as, according to the CDC, they will remove 95% Trusted Origin of airborne particles. N95 masks are often commonly used to paint or treat highly dangerous chemicals.

The breathers are chosen to suit your profile. They will shape a tight seal so that there are no holes in the airborne viruses. Health workers use it to protect them from infectious illnesses in the soil, such as hepatitis and anthrax.

Contrary to standard face masks, breathers shield against both big and tiny objects. Respirators masks are known to be much more effective than standard face masks by avoiding the flu virus. Nonetheless, tests have found benefits for all forms of masks.

DIY Face Masks May Be Effective

The WHO believes that the general population cannot be shielded from infectious diseases such as virus or influenza. Masks protect those who care for the ill and avoid the transmission of the illness if the ill are carried. Researchers at Hong

Kong Hospital, the Hong Kong Customer Council, and other organizations collaborated to determine the efficacy of surgical masks available for purchase and to create a strategy to make your face masks in shortages. The laboratory experiments found that the masks were 80% to 90% more effective than surgical masks when removing aerosol and droplets. Although these masks are not as effective as those you can purchase, the research team has carried out some strict tests and decided that three layers of effective masking are necessary:

The outer layer-The water-soluble coating must be used to avoid droplets. A tab for a plastic file fits well.

Middle layer-Filtration must be provided in this area. The team analyzed the paper towel using an electron microscope and determined that the structure was similar to that of a purchased mask.

Internal layer – This layer must remove water vapor from the person wearing the mask's breath. A facial tissue with three to four plies fits well.

FACE MASK PATTERNS

Please use tightly woven cotton such as quilting cotton when stitching a homemade face mask. Must do insure you wash and dry the fabric hot/high before cutting out bits and beginning to sew (bleach washing is usually a smart idea, too).

There are other face mask trends online, but these are the ones I've seen hospitals and related organizations. When you work with an agency, test if it guides you to a particular trend or needs different content, if you donate globally, you can see if you want to donate to a specific mask design in your organization.

Otherwise, you can use one of the following patterns: NOTE: it is very difficult to locate at this stage elastically, so I have marked the patterns below by using bands instead of elastic. Most of the designs use brace bias. You can buy prejudicial tape, but in fact, it is very easy to make your own from the same cloth you are using to make the mask (and it is cheaper because it is 100% cotton).

It has bands rather than rope, a pocket to connect a filter, and includes the (optional) wire to fit around the nose. This seems to be a MUCH Stronger choice for a template, but you will search anywhere you offer to see whether or not they want to install a cable.

The Turban Project/Deaconess Mask

This mask pattern was developed by the Turban movement and was provided by Deaconess Health Services to help people knit masks. This mask is incredibly easy to make-it begins with a rectangle of fabric, which is meant to mimic a surgical mask. You will find a video on the page explaining how to do it. I've already made a couple of these, and you probably can make everyone in about 15 minutes, if you have any sewing experience.

How to Make a Face Mask

What you will need

Cotton cover, the best thing is a beautiful print.

Elastic rope, elastic cord beading can work (you can even work us with 1/8 "flat elastic).
Cut off the 7 "elastic and tie a knot at either end (NOT knot the ends of the flat).

You can make two sizes: Adult or Child

Sheets o Cut 9x6 (Adult) or 7.5 x 5 (Child) on the right sides of the cotton cloth.
Sew to the first corner, avoid from the middle of the lower lip. Sew the elastic out onto the corner

with the lip. Several points forward and back hold this.

Sew to the next corner, stop and put the other end of the same elastic in the corner and stitch back and forth.

Then tie the mask over to the next corner. It also takes the tension out of the elastic. Thread the next corner and thread the same elastic at the other end.

Cut across the bottom and open around 1.5 "to 2." Don't cut yarn. Cut yarn. Turn inside out.

Transform inside out.

On either side of the mask pin 3 tucks. Check all the tucks are in the same direction.

Sew twice around the bottom of the head. It's too easy to do that. Make sure that every fabric style is horizontally oriented.

Sweet Red Poppy

This design is a perfect substitute, as it uses bias tape bands instead of elastic, and is very difficult to find. Bias Tape Mask This is the same basic style as the deaconess mask, but it also has a pocket that can be inserted into by the healthcare provider.

Supply List

100% Cotton Fat Quilting Quarters. Sewing machine.

Rotary cutter.

Cutting Mat for self-healing. Acrylic rule. Acrylic rule.

Sewing buttons.

Floral cable. Floral cable. Wire Cutters. Wire Cutters.

Cutting Chart

Quilting (Tightly Woven) Cotton 3 Layers:

Adult: 9″ x 7″ Child: 7″ x 5″
Cut 2 pieces of Double Fold 1/2″ Bias Tape 40″

Floral Wire 6″

Step 1. Pin Fabric
Bring two bits of cloth together on the opposite hands. Leave the third part for the stages two finish.

Place a pin in each corner of the rectangle and mark the middle of the rectangle horizontally.

Step 2. Sew Filter Pocket
A straight horizontal line 2-3′′ in length sewed halfway down from the top of the garment.

Repeat, on the other hand, leaving the middle unsewn.

Pinch the top two corners and bring them back to the bottom. Do the same on the rear skin. Place the last rectangle on top of the lining on each other's right side. Sew the short sides of the face mask to create a line of 3/8ths inch in the beginning and end of each pattern.

Step 3. Turn Fabric

Turn off the mask on the right side and press it flat with an iron. Be patient to smooth out the seams.

Step 4. Create Pin Tuck Markings
Create three-pin tuck points, fold the mask halfway, and press it with an iron. Then fold the exterior edges to the middle and then press again.

Step 5. Sew Bias Tape.
Open the bias ends and pull them back so that the right sides meet each other. Cut a straight line down the short end of the partition band to ensure the thread is protected. Turn right to a clean line. Turn right.

Find the middle of the bias tape and put it in the middle of the face. To match the raw edge of the bias tape with the raw edges of the mask, remove the bias tape. Pin in place along the mask length. Draw the inclination tape on the hollow nearest to the raw edge and repeat that on the other side.

You will face the filter slot away; it is situated on the back of the mask.

OPTIONAL
Cut a 5-6 "floral wire onto a compact section of the nose. Holding the ends of the wire inside to prevent slicing through the paper. Slide the wire into the bias strip in the center of the suit. Pins the floral tape on either side and lift it to prevent binding it.

Stretch the bias tape backward and enclose the raw side, thread and sew 1:4 of an inch from the bottom around the whole length of the bias tape. You will use your fingertips to direct the bias tape when you bind it.

Step 6. Create Pin Tucks
Make 1/2 "downward folds. Move the folds in order so that all tucks face the same way.

Step 7. Topstitch
Using a 3/8ths inch seam allowance thread, the pintucks around the right and left side of the whole mask.

Fu Face Mask

This is another basic mask pattern –This one has no flats but is angled to give decent facial coverage instead. The Fu Face Mask uses ties or rope so that it may be a nice choice.

Step 1: Join center seam
Enter the curved seam in the middle of our mask by stitching the positive side together.

Repeat this process both for the outer (main) and the internal (lining) fabrics.

Step 2 (optional): Press the center seam
This move has little practical value; it just increases the appearance of the mask. And if you're not worried, don't think about it.
Press the middle seam allowance open so that the seam lies smooth and comfortable.
It won't lie flat because it's a bent surface. So you should tackle it from one hand with the iron and then from the other hand with the second half. Instead, a personalized hem or pillow may be used to click.

Repeat this process both for the outer (main) and the internal (lining) fabrics.

Step 3: Sew the outer to the inner fabric and attach ribbons
We now stitch the inner (lining) fabric to the outer (main) fabric and patch the bond in one step.

Place the good side up on your lining thread. To attach two ribbons on the corners of one hand and mask a little out of the mask, but the rope bends inward.

Now place the key cloth with the positive side city on top of it. Now you should have all layers of the mask on top of each other with two ribbons between them.

Pin them through ribbons and fabrics to protect them. Then, on the other hand, do the same.

You should note that you will not have to pin it and can easily push the ribbons when you reach a corner.

Now stitch around the mask to hold one side open so that we can slip the mask off later.
Be vigilant not to trap any of the ribbons in the fabric, because you like them. Then direct them through the gap on one leg, or tie them between your layer masks to keep them out.

Step 4: Turn the mask inside-out
Your mask is now inside and turning it inside out means we take it on, or daily.
Only hold the left side open and take the mask carefully to turn it.

Step 5 (optional): Press the mask
This move has no practical value; it just enhances the look of your mask. And if you're not worried, don't think about it.
Now it's time to move the mask as it should be. Before this, ensure this will cover the edge of the side we left exposed within so that we press it flat as though it were sewn.

Step 6: Close open side of the mask and edge-stitch around the edge
Now it is time to cover our mask's side, which we left open to turn inside.
We won't only close the gap, but even the edge-stitch around the whole mask so that we can give our mask extra protection and leave the lining behind.

Carefully fold the open side inside, then sew the

edge around the whole head.

Step 7: Wear your mask or make a bunch That's; you're done! You're done! You should wear a mask now. Get a lot much bigger, and you can even offer other masks.

A.B. Face Mask

It has flats at the front and links around the top of the head and the bottom of the back. This pattern takes a little longer to make as the ties are connected but do appear to give a nice, comfortable match.

This pattern is planned for two purposes. First, completely over the nose, like an operative mask. Second, platters are modified so that the mask can suit several N-95 versions to create a safety shield in the hope of extending the respirator's life. After your change, the mask will and should be cleaned like your scrubs.
I suggest using a closely woven cloth. This pattern was produced with 100% cotton high quality. The trend is to render a mask of a fat quarter of tissue. I believe there are easier ways to cut large-scale manufacturing components.

Supplies:

A fat quarter of 100% cotton or other tightly woven material - the tighter, the better
Sewing machine Iron

Step 1: Print the Pattern
Take out the pattern. Cut plain black lines and green dotted lines.
Choose your fabric-21"x18 "at least (Fat Quarter). Brush out wrinkles. Draw out wrinkles.

Step 2: Fold Fabric
Right-side Fold cloth with jungle edge brush-taco design. Square fabric. Square cloth.

Step 3: Cut Binding and Ties
Split 5 x 1.5-inch long fabric width sheets. Each strip will have about 20 "length. The strips above are sliced into the half with the cloth folded. Or, if you take out the longer fabric, you can make 2 (1.5" wide x 40 "long) and 1 (1.5" wide x 20 "long), save yourself the binding together in one move.

Step 4: Refold Fabric and Cut Mask Face
Open and fold the remaining fabric. Fold width-wise-type burrito. So hem on the edges, fold on the bottom equally. The upper half of the folded cotton pin pattern. Dotted template line with fold alignment. Break along pattern tops. Cut the notches out.
Draw template and transfer to the lower half of the folded tissue. Cut the second piece out.

Step 5: Stack and Sew
Place the 2 bits of the face mask, face down. Pin in place. Cover all four sides with a 1/2 "edge.

Step 6: Iron in Pleats
With pointed (top hand) coming away from you,

bring the bottom side of the fabric up and down. The fold will be the imaginary line from top left to top right. Click hot iron crease. The flap is 1/4 inch.

Next, pull back the fabric. The fold will be a great line from right to left and to the center. Press the hot iron plunger. Third and fourth notches replicate.

The 5th (yellow headed pin) and 6th (red-headed pin) was replicated. Once the plates are ironed at the mask ends, weigh 3-give or take.

Step 7: Sew Pleats in Place
Sew plates with a 1/2-inch seam into place. Left and right sides of the mask face.

Step 8: Mark and Sew Darts
Split the face of the mask to half in the middle section. Front hand of cloth, the error of cloth facing you.

Place the top and bottom darts with a pen or pencil in a line pattern. Sew along the line. -- Just for good luck, and go over it.

Step 9: Trim Excess
Split edges up to 1/4 inch. Need to bind now!

Step 10: Prepare the Binding
Take 2 strips and 90-degree lock. Repeat on 2 strips more.
Put the strips together at an angle of 45 deg. Cut seams in 1/4 inch and press iron.
Grab the fourth strip and half it.

Step 11: Attach Side Binding
For the face mask faced down - face facing down, incorrect fabric facing up to you-pin 1.5 "tie, you cut half to the right and left of the mask. The binding must be face down. Binding edge matched for mask's end side. Thread in place, beginning from the top of the mask and ending just under mask using 1/4 of an inch of stitching.

Step 12: Finish Side Binding
Turn mask over. Turn mask off. The left hand of the cloth.

Fold 1/4 inch seam to you from the outward binding bottom. Wrap the bent lip across the mask's side slip.
Lock in place.
Sew around the linking point. On the other leg, repeat.
Excess trim.

Step 13: Attach Top/Bottom Binding
Pin 1.5-inch binding strips around the top and bottom edges with mask nose, fault facing you. Sew in contact with seams of 1/4 inch. Begin stitching just above one side of the face of the mask and stop directly after the opposite ear. Press iron open.

Step 14: Finish Top/Bottom Binding and Ties And on both sides of the mask trim ties.
Iron on top and bottom of mask ties in 1/4 inch row. Iron on the end of mask ties in 1/4 inch row.

Fold the ties in a piece in half and hold. Sew Binding and Hold Bound.

Step 15: Done and Done! Congratulations! You're done! You're done! You made a mask that protects a helpless patient.

I encourage you now to make a different one and then another. And make any of your mates. If you have a dozen or more people, contact the nearest hospital, speak to the emergency department, and agree to drop them off (6 feet or more safe).

INSTRUCTIONS FOR HOMEMADE FACE MASK (WITH ELASTIC)

Materials needed (with elastic)

Soft cloth of cotton (i.e., cotton).

Fabric must be freshly bought and rarely used within around the last year.

Wash and dry cloth before stitching with no color or dyes. Rope Elastic is the work that can be performed using an elastic beading cord (you can use even a 1/8 "flat elastic if it is inaccessible 1/4").

One adult mask needs two (2) 9"x6 "tight-woven cotton pieces and two 7" 1/4 "elastic pieces.

Therefore, a 44 "wide yard creates 12-15 masks. For 25 masks, it takes 7.5 yards of elastic (14 inches per mask).

You can make two sizes: Adult or Child. Adult-sized masks will be the greatest need.

Cut 9x6 (adult) or 7.5x5 (child) into the right sides of the cotton fabric (to make sure the pattern style is horizontal).

Sew to the first corner, avoid from the middle of the bottom lip. Sew the elastic out onto the corner with the lip. A lot of points forward and back are going to keep this.

Sew to the next corner, pause and put a few stitches forward and back on the other side of the same elastic corner.

Then tie the mask over to the next corner. Bring the elastic out again with the lip.

Next to the next corner and stitch with the same elastic on the other edge.

Sew through the bottom, leaving roughly 1.5 "to 2" open. Stop, cut yarn. Transform inside out.

On either hand of the mask, pin 3 tucks. Ensure all the tucks are in the same direction.

Sew twice around the bottom of the head.

Facemask instructions: supplies needed: 1/8 to 1/4 inch flat elastic materials and 100% cotton cloth bought and never used in the last year.

Wash and rinse fabrics (no color or dyes) before stitching. One adult mask requires two 9 by 6-inch cloth rectangles and two 7-inch elastic pieces. A 44-inch long cloth- yard creates 12 to 15 masks. For 25 masks (14 inches per mask), you require yards of elastic.

Bring the right cloth sides together. Cut from 9 to 6 inches (adult) or 7.5 to 5 inches (child).

Sew to the first corner from the middle of the bottom edge, stop. Sew elastic out into the corner with the lip. Several stitches back and forth catch this. Clamp to the next corner, switch and carry the other end of the same elastic to the corner. Sew the mask out to the next corner. Elastic location with bottom out.

Next to the next corner and stitch with the same elastic on the other edge. Sew the rim, leaving about 11/2 to 2 inches open. End. Stop. Turn inside out. Turn inside out.

Add three tucks on each side of the mask in the same direction. Sew twice around the bottom of the head.

INSTRUCTIONS FOR HOMEMADE FACE MASK (NO ELASTIC NEEDED)

Materials needed

Tight-weave cotton cloth (e.g., quilting thread)
Tissue will be obtained freshly, never recycled, during the last year.
Wash and dry cloth before stitching with no color or dyes. Ties alternatives.
Bias tape (as available 1/2 or 7/8).

OR

Make ties on the above-stated fabric strips (cut strips 2 "width by 16" long).
Each adult mask needs two (2) 9"x6 "tight cotton bits and four
16" biased ties (64 "total per mask). Therefore, a 44 "wide yard creates 12- masks. For 12 masks, you need 21 1/3 meters of inclined tape. You can make two sizes: Adult or Child. Adult-sized masks will be the greatest need.

Bring together the right sides of the cotton fabric

(note that every fabric pattern is horizontal.) Sew along the edges of the cloth, leaving about 1.5 "to 2" free from the middle of the bottom edge.

Stop, cut yarn. Fiber removed. Turn inside out. Transform inside out.

On either side of the shield, pin three (3) 1/2 "tucks. Ensure all the tucks are in the same direction.

Bind with Bias Tape or Cotton.

Bias tape: closed loop.

Tissue: fold in half, switch under 1/4, 'iron on each side, thread the lengths of the edges tight, pin one (1) bind at each end, sew the bias twice along the mask edge and grab the bias tape as you go.

Resources needed above. Replace 1/2 or 7/8-inch bias tape or make bonds of 2-inch bands wide by 16-inch long.

One adult mask includes a cloth of two 9 by 6 inches and a bias tapestry of four 16 inches (total 64 inches per mask). For 12 masks, you need 21 1/3 meter bias tape.

Place cotton cloth right sides together and weigh as above. Sew along the edges of the cloth, from the middle of the bottom side, leaving between 1 1/2 to 2 inches free. Turn inside out. Turn inside out.

On each side of the mask, pin three 1/2-inch tucks, as above.

Create connections with tapestry or silk. Stitch bias tape in half, switch below 1/4 inch on each side and iron in place. Stitch bias paper tight. Broadsides of the thread closed.

Add one tie at either corner or stitch around the mask's edge twice; catch the bias tape as you go.

DIY MEDICAL FACE MASKS TO SEW

Medical face masks are unavailable. Hospitals need facial masks urgently for medical professionals. Once you stay home and learn how to crochet, your time and skills will be used for the better by sewing fabric face masks and donating them to the local hospital. We're going to craft for a cause!

Face masks can be made from finely knit 100% cotton cloth of good quality. Note that some men and women use them, and they enjoy a variety of colors and shapes.

Tissue face masks do not replace nasal facial masks with a professional category. But, owing to the lack, other hospitals use them in non-critical hospital areas or have a medical-grade mask.

Medical Face Mask with Ties

It is my favorite pattern developed by a nurse, as it does not need elasticity. Nurses claim they favor tie masks because they are flexible for longer times rather than elastic and more convenient to wear.

Face Mask with Elastic Loops

This is the most common design for the medical face, with two elastic loops flowing across the mouth. You can navigate this sequence if you are a novice. It provides a video tutorial for each move.

Center Seam Shaped Face Mask

This mask has side elastic ear clips, but the textiles are cut into an ergonomic shape to fit better over the nose rather than a straight cap. It also has a compartment for slipping a surgical mask into it. This design is also available in various sizes for children and adults.

Face Mask With Flexible Nose and Bias Tape Ties
This mask would actually be the most comfortable to use for healthcare staff,

as it incorporates a bendable wire in the nose to help preserve the form and bias tape ties to make it secure.

Face Mask Picture Tutorial

The face mask is contrasted around the two outer edges, supplying the mask with a good finish and potentially helping to keep the elastic tight.

Button Counter Face Mask
This mask is very similar to the deaconess mask and simple to make. It's perfect if you choose a LOTS of sample images written tutorial to a

video.

Materials needed:

piece of cloth 8 "x 14" I will prefer a non-directional print before you get acquainted with this tutorial. One with a scattered image written on the surface as seen.

sheets of 1.75 "(1 3/4") x 6 "cloth It is the accent of the edge. It may be the same cloth as the main component or a thin or solid print. Two bits are measuring 1/4 "elastic diameter. These are roughly 6 1/2 "tall.

Form for Ruler Manufacture branding. Pins. P Scissors.

Machine for sewing, threaded.

Fold the central fabric piece together in two, right sides. Sew down the bottom of the 8-inch diameter with a line of 1/4 inch.
Turn the tube shape inside out, and now on the outside the right side of the cloth. Place this flat and retain the groove on the smooth tube at one end.

Place the cloth tube so that the raw edges are on both sides and that the hem edge is on the bottom. Measure and measure a line 1 1/2 inches from the bottom edge with a ruler. Create another 1 "line above the base, about 2 1/2 inches from the bottom of the surface.

Do not use a pencil as you can see in the

illustration; use a stylus or a chalk paper. For comparison purposes, I used a pencil.

Fold the edge of the seam up (or down in this photo, as I flipped it upside down ... sorry) to make the first line plug. You will have an angle of 1 1/2 inch.

Flip over the tube bit. Compare the dotted edge to the second line you used to create. Write. Press. The plate you have just built is 1/2 inch deep. Push the plate down at each end of the raw edge.

You are now going to mark the lines for the second pleat. Label a 1/2 "line from the top of the last pleat (or 2" from the bottom edge of the seam). The top of the hollow in this photo was difficult to see, so look at the finger symbol above.

So mark an inch above the last line (or 3 inches over the seam edge). Follow the steps you have taken to render the first appeal with these lines as your reference.

Now you should have two folds, each 1/2 inch long. Repeat steps you used to make the second pleat so that you have a minimum of three folds.

Add one elastic element to the raw side, make sure it doesn't curl until it is stitched to the bottom at both ends. I put my 1/8 "from the top and bottom of the key folded piece. Secure in the rugged edge elastic 1/8 "inch. Move the remainder of the elastic component on the other raw side.

Place the band over the elastic. Make sure the raw edge faces out, and the hollow edge faces the main body of the plucked part. It'll take a little longer on the top and bottom, and that's all right because we'll fold it to the back. Lock in line both fabrics.

Trim the other end of the accent strip so that the bottom edge of the central plaster section is around 1/2 "wider.

Fold the bottom of the accent fabric strip to the wall, exactly as you did on the edges. Pin finishes all in place.

Use a 1/4 inch hem supply, stitch the whole edge line, ensuring that the thread is right at the beginning and end.

Open the seam of the accent strip by pulling it out of the central plissed section and press it.

Old slice with the Whole accent down into the key piece, exposing the bare surface. You can now see the focus on this leg, not on the opposite side, after least. Write. Write. Down the pin bottom.

You should change your pressing foot into a straight stitch foot if you are a good sewist. When you're slow, like me, you're going to leave the 1/4 "presser foot on your computer and take the next move. Stitch this accent strip down to the mask's main body, add the bottom, and secure the back of stitch at the beginning and end.

It is not a required move. This gives a good polished feel and makes it a bit more elastic support. Stitch the mask edge on the elastic leg.

You will now have a recyclable, washable, 4′′ x 7′′ (unopened) cap.

Enjoy!

P.S. The elastic range will naturally be tailored to the facial measurements.

Craft Passion Face Mask

This mask design is available in 4 sizes and uses elastic hair links to cover the head. This uses a contoured fit over the nose instead of tiles.

Material:

Tools

Main cloth, 13 "x 7", prewash.
Designed of cotton or flannel, twelve inches x 7, "prewash.
Elastic cord for 16 "or shoelace/ribbon/cord ear loops with a length of at least 44" for head attach.

Sewing patterns Face Mask; Choose the option

to import and print individually.

Sewing essential
Sewing Machine or hand sew
Iron
Seamstress tracing wheel and paper
Pencil or soluble fabric marker
Instructions

Pin the designs on the cloth, draw the cloth bits, and cut them out.
Sew, snap on the right side of the panel, turn the face mask on. Topstitch. Pin.
Sew the face mask mouth. Place the elastic cord in the rear pocket.

Cut settings are as follows:
Printed cotton fabric (like the fabric used for making quilts)
Cameo 4
Tool 2
Rotary blade
Force 15
Passes 1
Speed 8

I hope and pray that manufacturers will create masks of the medical quality that our health practitioners require! Meanwhile, sewing personalized face masks for use as a last resort is something I can do to help you in this tough moment.

WHEN TO WEAR A FACE MASK

Try wearing a face mask when you are coughed or sneezed in (with or without fever) when you plan to be with others. The face mask serves to shield them from the disease. Medical facilities have unique guidelines for wearing face masks.

When There is a Haze Period

Under the MOH FAQS on the Haze Health Warning, when air quality is expected to be within the Hazardous range (PSI>300), a safe person who needs to be outside for many hours should use a mask to minimize exposure. It is advised that disabled persons stop or limit physical exercise while the air quality outlook is extremely dangerous (PSI > 200). If they have to be outdoors for a few hours, visibility can be minimized by wearing an N95 mask. The elderly, pregnant women, and those with serious lung or cardiac conditions or trouble breathing should inform their doctor on the use of the mask N95. For brief exposure, N95 masks are not needed, such as moving from home to school or work, from bus stops to the Shopping Mall. N95 masks are also not required indoors.

When You Are Sick

When you are vomiting, coughing, or sneezing, tiny droplets of saliva and mucus containing infectious viruses are released into the air. These viruses will spread to your neighbors and even make them ill.

The wearing of an operating mask is one way to keep germs from transmitting to you when you feel nervous. A well-used mask prevents droplets from entering the skin as you cough or sneeze.

How to put on and remove a face mask
Disposable face masks can be thrown into the landfill now and only. If they are wet, you can always clean and replace masks.

Ignore company instructions also on mask usage and storage, and methods for putting on and removing a mask. If instructions are not available to put and remove the mask, then follow the steps below.

How to put on a face mask

Clean your hands before touching the mask with soap and water or a hand sanitizer.

Take a mask from the packaging to make sure the cracks or defects are not visible on either side of the mask.

Determine the top half of the suit. The part of the mask with a solid bendable bottom is the top, which is designed to shape the face. Determine the front face of the suit. Typically, the colored side of the mask is the front, which will turn you away while the white side covers your nose.

Follow the instructions below for the type of mask you are using.

Earloops face mask: keep the mask by the ear loops. Place a circle around the ear.

Face mask with ties: Bring the mask to your nose and lock the links over your head's crown. Face mask with strips: keep the mask with the neckpiece or top of the mask at the wrists so that the front strips can hang between your hands quickly. Bring the mask over your nose and draw the top strap around your ear over rest on your head's crown. Draw the lower strap over your head to rest on your back.

Mold or pinch the stiff edge to the shape of your nose.

If using a face mask with ties: Then take the bottom ties, one in each hand, and secure with a bow at the nape of your neck.
Pull the bottom of the mask over your mouth and chin. How to remove a face mask

Clean your hands before touching the mask with soap and water or a hand sanitizer. Stop hitting the mask edge. The mask front is dirty. Just touch the ears/band. Take the following instructions for the sort of mask you use.
Ear Loops face mask: hold all ear loops and raise the mask gently.

Face mask with ties: First untie the bottom arch and untie the top arch and pull off the mask while the ties are loosened.

Bands Face Mask: first, lift the lower strap over your head and slip the top strap over your ear. Throw in the garbage the mask. Clean your hands with water and soap or hand sanitizer.

PROPER FACE MASK USE

In its 2016 "Dental Review of Infection Control Activities," the USA. CDC advises dentistry practitioners should use their eyes, nose, and eye safety for operations that are likely to cause blood splashes or sprays or other bodily fluids. It is important to note that, in the Hierarchy of Exposure Controls, personal protective equipment (PPE) such as face masks are the last. That means that it is essential to concentrate on other control methods before we put a facial mask on in the evening. For example, procedures during this pandemic were told not to treat patients with signs of respiratory illness.

Of note, face masks are a required part of any dental treatment given more restrictions. Sadly, bad face mask habits among dentists are popular. Yet bad practices propagate quickly like viruses. Hygienists and other dentists prefer to take their recommendations from those from whom they work.

Below are a few successful facial mask practices for dentistry, beginning with choosing the correct mask for the job at hand.

Know How Masks Are Classified and Rated
N95 respirators, which have been reviewed, tested, and certified by the National Institute for

Occupational Safety and Health (NIOSH), are typically the top quality masks recommended for use in dental environments. N95 breathers filter at least 95% of the contaminants in the air and are forbidden for use in patients with or suspected of respiratory illness. Nevertheless, most dental procedures do not need N95 respirators, but maybe in medical therapy-diagnosis with adequate triages should be deferred until later on after patients have sufficiently stabilized from signs of respiratory diseases.

The American Society for Research and Materials (ASTM) sets standards of consistency and the components that are most commonly used in dental conditions of the face masks. The standards measure fluid resistance, performance in bacterial filtration, submicron particulate filtration performance, differential pressure and flame propagation. Each mask earns a ranking according to its level of safety, in compliance with the ASTM standards.

The ASTM evaluations are optional, but they are carried out by the top dental mask manufacturers. The ASTM F2100-11 specification includes a graphical representation of the mask output rating on the package.
Watch for packaging saying anything like "grade 2" may mean that the manufacturer did not personally check the masks.

Wear Your Mask Right-Side-Up and Right-Side-Out

A dental mask should have three layers: the outer layer is moisture resistant, the middle layer cleans, and the inner layer covers the nose. The textures inside and outside are not identical.
Dental practitioners wear their masks more inside than you might expect. If the masks are color-coded, the contrast between the inside and the outside is easy to see. Review the manufacturer's instructions for non-color-coded masks. Furthermore, manufacturers usually pack their masks face up with the outside.

Dental facial masks should suit the face's contours. Laps between your skin and a mask's edge can allow pollutants to enter. Your face mask must be focused on correctly.
Like a waterfall, the flaps on a face mask will face down.

A face mask may offer extra protection against sickness. The CDC advises, however, that you use masks only if you are advised by a doctor or if you have respiratory symptoms, to prevent infection for others around you. There are no known threats beyond the expense of purchasing these products.

Don (Put On) Your Mask Correctly

Some people make the error as they place their masks over their heads first. But before you securing your mask, make a small indentation or divot on your nose piece with your thumb. It

helps better to place the mask on the bridge of the nose.
Open it a bit when you donate the mask (but not so much that the folds flicker). It makes the mask a perfect fit.

Using your index and middle finger to form the nose piece between your eyes and the bridge of your nose after you have looped your mask over your mouth. This contoured fit helps shield a clinician's face in the most polluted area.
Then stretch the mask around the mouth and chin full. If you have a Stable Fit TM mask, change the bottom chin strap. This secures the exterior edges of the mask around the face and offers 360 degrees of security.
Remove your glasses before you place your mask if you have lenses. After your mask, put your glasses on.

Don’t Twist the Ear Loops Into Figure Eights
Often, practitioners with a broader face structure find like their masks are not adequately secure. They shorten the ear loops to compensate by making them into figure eight.
The concern is that the mask material is held up to the mouth and nose. Breath condensation travels inside the mask and allows the fibers of the mask material to swell in a process called wicking. In effect, this weakens the mask's ability to trap microbes. Using a Safe Fit mask is the best fit.

Take Off Your Mask Correctly

Much when there is a way to put on a face mask, there is a way to remove one. Incorrect removal of a tooth mask may lead to cross-contamination. Remember that the exterior surface of a face mask is coated with a film of aerosols, bacteria, blood bleeding and saliva. Place your fingertips under each ear loop above your ear lobes to make a face mask and pull straight back. Then remove the mask from the forehead and wash it. Should not contact the mask and use a mask even in the treatment room. Wash or using alcoholic hand rub shortly after the removal of the mask.

Although masks seem to be promising, other prevention steps are also necessary. Make sure you always wash your hands — especially if you are

with people who may be ill. Make sure that the yearly influenza shot prevents you and others from transmitting the infection.

Can Wearing A Face Mask Protect You From The New Coronavirus?

A new coronavirus, dubbed SARS-CoV-2, can be covered by a more advanced mask known as the respirator N95. The respirator is safer than the surgical mask, but it is not approved for general use, at least not at this stage by Schaffner or the Centers for Disease Prevention and Control (CDC).
It's, in part, that it's uncomfortable to wear

these masks for long stretches, he said. Specialists are instructed regularly on how to match these respirators properly around the nose, lips and mouth, making sure the wearers do not breathe around the edge of the respirator. "When you do that, it turns out that ventilation practice is difficult because you are moving into the really heavy stuff. You have to breathe in and out. It's a bit claustrophobic.

"I know that when I need about half an hour, I can wear them," he said. "I will leave the insulation area, take it off and take a few deep breaths to cool off before I can go back inside,"

Schaffner recommended that although it might still be possible to snack an N95 respirator online. When so many people load up excessively respirators, the wellbeing of emergency staff and those who use them could be put in risk, Schaffner said. Schaffner said.

FACE MASK VS. RESPIRATOR

If you've ever been to the dentist, the surgical masks look familiar — medical practitioners use them to avoid liquid splashing into their mouths. They fit loose and invite airborne particles into them. Across East Asian countries, people usually wear face masks to shield themselves from smog and respiratory diseases, but they are not equipped to block minute particles from the air.

The main purpose of a face mask is to prevent fluid from reaching the mouth or nose of an infected person's sneeze or cough (gross, I know). Using one will defend you from illness if you are in close contact with someone who is infected and help prevent you from transmitting the disease to someone else. Wearing it around sick patients is a common practice in medical professions.

Face masks can also help prevent transfers of the hand to the head because you cannot contact your mouth directly while using one. Nevertheless, viruses can be spread through the nose or eyes, and virologists agree that surgical facial masks cannot block infectious viruses from reaching the body.

You will need a breather, a safe fitting tool worn around the nose. If you say "respirator," you usually mean the N95 respirator, which is called after at least 95 percent of the small particles removed. Some manufacturers offer N95 breathers which come in all sizes. Make aware that the packaging says "N95" when shopping for these sorts of mask-Most masks will just call them "respirator," but if they are not called N95, you do not get the maximum standard of security.

Dr. Michael Hall, a CDC vaccine vendor, announced in an e-mail that N95 breathable aircraft are most safe, but surgical masks are used to shield you from other people's coughs. N95 masks are difficult to put on, so be sure to see a tutorial or see a guide on how to suit your face. Hall says the key is to wear the mask over the mouth and nose without any holes. Just keep it on once — a respirator that is only used is not nearly as effective often.

A government-approved N95 mask will potentially lower the risk of viral diseases, but it is the most reliable way to protect yourself with the simple preventive activities recommended by the medical and scientific community.
If you have no access to an N95 mask and require one to shield people from your disease, and the operative face mask would be sufficient. But, as noted, if you wear a face mask, you will get less protection from airborne viruses. Hall says that you can also tie a scarf or other cotton fabric around your nose and lips.

Respirators

Respirators are designed to reduce the respiratory radiation of a person. Respirators come in different sizes and must be selected uniquely to match the face of the wearer to provide a transparent screen. The proper filtering between the skin of the patient and the respirator allows the air to be drawn through the filter content of the respirator and not through gaps between the face and respirator.

Respiratory Infection Control: Respirators Versus Surgical Masks

Surgical Masks
Surgical masks are used as a physical wall to protect the patient from harmful situations such as huge droplets of blood or bodily fluids. Surgical masks also shield people from contamination by using the surgical mask. These masks capture large body fluid spores, which may contain bacteria or wearer viruses. Surgical masks are used for a number of applications, including:

Sick people are placed to limit the spread of contagious respiratory secretions to others. Worked by practitioners for the avoidance of accidental contamination of bacteria usually found in mucus and saliva of patients 'wounds. Staff can also hold infected fingers/hands-off mouth and nose in order to protect themselves from sprinkling or shower of blood or body fluids.

Surgical masks are not equipped or approved to prevent minor airborne particles from being inhaled. Such contaminants are not visible to the human eye but can also cause infection. Surgical masks are not designed to cover the user's face carefully. Many of the potentially polluted air will flow through holes between the face and the surgical mask during inhalation, not be drawn through the mask's filter content. Their ability to remove small particles vary considerably due to the type of substance used to produce the surgical mask, meaning that staff cannot be counted on to protect against airborne infectious agents. Just surgical masks approved by the United States. The U.S. Food and Drug Administration has been tested for its ability to withstand blood and body fluids.

N95 masks fit your face and go through a certification

As they build a tight bond between respiratory masks and the skin that helps remove at least 95% of the airborne particulate matter, N95 respirator masks vary from other forms of surgical masks and face masks. They may include an exhalation valve that makes breathing more comfortable when wearing it. Coronavirus may be spread by mist (breath) and coughing, sneezing, saliva, and transmission over regularly touched surfaces for up to 30 minutes.

Each N95 mask model is accredited by the National Institute for Occupational Safety and Health by each manufacturer. N95 OR Masks are approved by the Food and Drug Administration for surgical use via secondary approval-they better protect patients from access to contaminants such as patient blood.

N95 masks must also pass a compulsory fitness test in American care facilities using a standard developed by OSHA, the Occupational Safety and Health Administration before they are used. This video by maker 3 M (linked) illustrates some of the main variations between ordinary operative masks and N95 masks.

Who Handmade Masks Are For

Hospitals and emergency facilities take unusual steps to replenish their supplies and accept voluntary donations with items such as N95 goggles, safety glazing and nitrile gloves. Many people who ask for hand-sewn masks

remember that the masks issued would go to concerned patients and nonclinical staff, not doctors and nurses.
In other clinics and emergency centers, disposable gear is so limited that they can only use surgical masks or other masks if there is no other alternative. Several health centers recommend their favorite designs and suggest that masks have four cloth layers to trap particles better. Officials are asked to show a high degree of vigilance in such situations.

Homemade Masks Aren't Sterilized
Factory-made masks from companies such as 3 M, Kimberly-Clark and Prestige Ameritech are certified and are known to be sterile out of the hospital case. With homemade face masks, the mask is not sterile or clean of a coronavirus environment.

The CDC finds N95 masks polluted after each use and advises that they are discarded. Nevertheless, due to the severe lack of N95 masks, many hospitals have taken drastic steps to protect physicians and nurses, such as attempting to decontaminate masks between uses. For e.g., one medical center in Nebraska experiments with ultraviolet therapy to sterilize N95 masks.

The Danger: Not Knowing The Limits

There is no risk to yourself if you still want to design your own face masks for personal use because it gives you a challenge and peace of mind. But the mask is essential to understand because you cannot dramatically reduce your chances of having coronavirus by making your own face mask, mainly if you are interested in risky behaviors such as going to crowded locations.

As the coronavirus can be spread by someone who is free of symptoms and indeed has the virus, it is vital to the health and wellbeing of people over 65 years of age, and those underlying conditions for understanding the proven interventions can help to safeguard everybody.

THE BASICS OF SURGICAL MASK SELECTION

The problem of hospital infection prevention is a regular challenge for both health staff members and patients. Surgeons, anesthetists, nurses, and infection control professionals have educated views and individual convictions on the causes and avoidance of infection in the clinical setting. It has to be done to remove or at least reduce infection causative agents is a problem for all.

The history of surgery and the cap, dressing, and masking procedures dates back to the 1860s. Live microorganisms are thought to be extracted from the blood, bare skin, and mucus membranes. Studios by Tuneval in Great England suggested that the use of operational masks does not affect the number of possible pathogenic bacteria in the air near the site of the operation, and question the value of the use of surgical masks1. While there is no evidence to suggest that masks are not necessary for reducing wound infections, surgical masks are used in throughout recent years, the safety of the healthcare professional and the patient has become a question in infection control and is becoming increasingly complex. Some of the problems relating to the real need to wear an operating mask in the surgical area (OR) are controlled.

Health professionals may wear a mask and eye protection or facial shield to protect mucous membranes of the head, nose and mouth during operations and patient care practices likely to generate blood, corporal fluids, secretions, or excretions splashes or sprays.

Transmission-based precautions are advised in the treatment of patients with highly transmissible or epidemiologically significant infections evidence or potential infection, or where specific measures other than standard measures are required.
Droplet precautions: a surgical mask is typically used to guard against large bacterial particles that are spread by direct contact, and can only move small distances (up to 3

feet) from coughing and sneezing sick patients. If prone individuals enter the rooms of patients confirmed or suspected of having measles (rubeola) or chickenpox, then respiratory security will be given to them.
FDA. FDA. Medical devices are governed by the Food and Drug Administration (FDA). Section 201(h) of the Federal Food, Drug and Cosmetic Act describes a medical product. The definition includes any article intended for use in human-made remedies, reduction, diagnosis, or prevention of disease that does not accomplish its intended purposes by means of chemical intervention or is based on metabolism (e.g., a medicinal substance). An example of an item regulated as a medical device is a surgical mask.

NIOSH. NIOSH. NIOSH is a federal agency and branch of the Department of Health and Human Services, which identifies substances that pose potential health problems and recommends limits on exposure to OSHA. NIOSH carries out comprehensive protection, and health studies provide technical assistance and propose criteria for OSHA adoption. NIOSH also certifies ventilation gear.

Masks are often worn in the OR, where sterile supplies are delivered, in clean cores, and at scrub sinks. Whenever blood splashing, spray or aerosol, or other potentially contagious materials may be created, masks with face guards and masks and protective eyewear are required. The healthcare staff typically wear a face mask to protect against the transmission of large-particle droplets produced in direct contact and usually only fly short distances (up to 3 feet) from sick patients who cough or sneeze. The OSHA Blood Borne Pathogen Standard (BBPS) (29 CFR 1910.1030) requires the use of goggles, eye scapes, and face covers under specific circumstances to reduce the risk of bloodborne pathogens exposure. In December 1991, this regulation was released. The aim of BBPS is to remove or decrease worker access to bloodborne pathogens such as hepatitis B (HBV) and HIV. This requires standardized protocols, risk preparation, patient screening, vaccine and medication standards, safety reviews, workplace conditions, identification, and personal protective equipment issued by employers. The BBPS:

Needs a mask used for eye shielding or a chin-length facial protector to be used while conditions for blood contact and other highly contagious body fluids or materials occur.
It requires a face mask to prevent the passage of blood or other infectious body fluids to the skin, eyes, mouth, or other mucous membranes of employees under regular splashing and spraying conditions.

Masks with different characteristics can be found in various forms and picked for personal security and design and fitness preferences. The most popular styles in the workroom are perfect tie-on, duckbill, cone-shaped, flat-folded with shields, and duckbill with shields. High fluid-resistant ear loop covers are also available that can be used by roaming nurses in the OR. Masks are only successful if they are correctly worn. Masks minimize the flow from the wearer of infectious pieces to the atmosphere and help shield the wearer from splashing or splashing of blood and body fluid. Masks would be secure, protecting both the mouth and the nose. Workers in the sterile area should use a face mask or clear eyewear. The design will ensure that there is no tenting on the sides of the mouth to spread or encourage bacteria to enter. A narrow folding strip on the nose would match similarly. Masks should be periodically adjusted and damp at all moments. When the mask is removed, treat the strings only and immediately discharge them into a waste bin. This is not uncommon for masks to be put beneath the nose or moistened with blood or body fluids. A mask should never hang or peddle around the face, nor should it be folded and inserted in a pocket for later use.

EFFECTIVENESS OF SURGICAL MASKS

Few tests have demonstrated the efficacy of surgical masks for sterile field safety. The focus on the safety of the patient during the procedure in the production of operation masks to date has, therefore, been focused on filtering capacity and has been calculated in various ways (Belkin, 1997). The efficacy of mask filter aggregation is highly subjective. Tests have shown varying levels of penetration based on particle size and the research methods employed (Cooper et al., 1983b; Tuomi, 1985; Brosseau et al., 1997; McCullough et al., 1997; Willeke and Qian, 1998). Two reports suggest that the wearing of a mask has little effect on the occurrence of surgical wound infection (Orr, 1981; Tunevall, 1991). One research found that wearing masks under headgear inhibits the minimization of face seal leakage (Ha'eri and Wiley, 1980).

Non-Surgical Masks and Alternative Materials
In addition to FDA-approved medical masks, some look or tissue cotton masks are available.

During the epidemic of Extreme Acute Respiratory Syndrome (SARS) in Asia, masks of this type were widely used (see Chapter 3). In fact, in emergency situations, staff and the public have sometimes covered their airways with ready-to-use items (such as sheets or towels) or with unapproved plastic facemasks, sold as respiratory aid in hardware shops.
New reusable surgical masks were made of woven fabric that only separated air from the surgical wound. In the early 1960s, surgical masks often made from cheesecloth were replaced with the synthetic materials mentioned previously, providing both increased filtration performance and bacterial filtration.
Specific mannequin research has shown that these fabrics can minimize aerosol particulate amounts and some water-soluble gasses and vapors at pressure decrease suitable to breathe in accident situations. In tandem with innovative facial fit methods (e.g., nylon hose), leaking can be minimized (Cooper et al. 1983b). The animal tests indicate that carefully designed six- layer gauze masks decrease the occurrence of tuberculosis bacilli infection by 90% to 95% (Lurie and Abramson 1949). Regulatory standards ensure,

however, that a mask does not allow blood or other potentially contagious products, under usual operating circumstances and for the duration of time the protective equipment is being used, to move or touch the wearer's face, head, or mouth or other mucous membranes (OSHA, 1992).

LEARN THE PROS AND CONS OF USING A DIY FACE MASK TO HELP WITH ACNE

Acne is one of the worst factors that can harm our skin and is not only limited to adolescents. Surprisingly, acne affects many people every day, and there is a full beauty industry that seeks to cure this condition, from facial masks to foundations. Naturally, different natural strategies can appear enticing to attempt to keep your face transparent, and one of these is to keep a facial mask. Like often, there are benefits and drawbacks of using acne natural facial masks. It used to be exclusive to the day spa has now come to our baths and daily rituals, and several different natural masks are available on the market. There is almost everything you can think of from charcoal to honey to cover your hair, and most of those things are natural. You want to step back and examine your acne problem before deciding on a specific natural face mask; is it wrong? You may want to figure out whether the acne condition is caused by dry skin or even everyday dirt and grit. A mask does not do you any good if you will not take the other measures to exfoliate and cleanse your face, and that is why many therapies for counter acne fail. We will take a look at the benefits and drawbacks of using one of the different natural face masks to tackle the acne problem.

Pro: A Natural Face Mask Will Open Your Pores
One of the principal culprits behind acne is the obstruction of your pores. Whether it's dirt or oily skin, the outcome is still trapped, so you will want to cleanse your face many times daily. A decent washing mask opens your pores and extracts any debris from them, leaving your skin with a thoroughly cleaner feeling and look. Of course, using a face mask is not the only way you want to combat acne, but it can be a significant first step in the battle against clear skin.

Con: Overexposure Can Cause A Rash
Like most good things, too much good can cause you a problem, and the same can be said with the facial masks for time. You won't remove the face mask for long because prolonged exposure will create a bad skin rash. The

skin rash is particularly a drawback if you attempt to combat acne in that way, and if you have a facial mask, it takes time to read the instructions, and following the time limits is an essential part of the proper application of the mask.

Pro: No Chemical Burns

There are some significant benefits when it comes to treating acne, and one of them is that you do not suffer any chemical burns. Many counter-acne remedies tend to flame the skin if they are not applied correctly, and that is sadly the path the acne industry has taken toward the full treatment of acne. Still, without risking a fire, a natural mask will cleanse your face and exfoliate your pores. The natural approach would be perfect if you love holistic beauty treatments and want to prevent rash for your face.

Con: A Natural Face Mask Might Not Work For All Acne Cases

Here's the thing, acne will have her own mind. The typical path does not even work with the most difficult situations or other forms of acne. Usually, this is when acne regulation comes into play, and there are several explanations that an acne case may be so serious. Hormones appear to make our skin split up very much and can cause acne levels to fluctuate on our skin, where there is a hormone imbalance. While this is unpleasant, there won't be too many appropriate natural solutions for this.

Acne Can Be Controlled With The Right Mixture Of Treatments

Perhaps nothing that is so physically and mentally fragile as acne, because your beauty is such an essential part of your self-esteem. It can be a difficult battle to get your acne under control, and often the counter-remedies are either not an effective option or are just too strong. A natural face mask may be a far more effective option, if you are tired of the drying out of your face, to help keep your skin tall and potentially remove your acne problem in a much more enjoyable manner.

Considerations In The Use Of Homemade Masks To Protect Against Virus

Homemade masks may include those that are:
Made of linen, cotton, for example.
Attach other masks or filters into pockets.
Be worn on breathers N95 (in an effort to reuse breathable).

Homemade masks are not medical appliances and are thus not regulated, such as surgical masks and respirators. There are a number of drawbacks to their use:

They have not been checked in compliance with recognized criteria.

They cannot have complete protection against the particulate matter of virus size.
The edges of the nose and mouth are not built to create a barrier.

Bacteria are not similar to those found in surgical masks or respirators.

They can be hard to breathe, though, and they can keep you from having the amount of oxygen your body needs.

These will need regular modification, increase the touch of your hands with your face, and increase the risk of infection.

Such masks cannot be used to remove fragments of the infection that can be spread by coughing, sneezing, or other surgical procedures. They will not have complete protection against coronavirus due to their inherent loose fit and materials.

Just N95 operating breathable (not surgical masks) fit-tested NIOSH- approved are intended to offer maximum safety. Such respirators are Health Canada licensed medical equipment. An N95 respirator is a respiratory safety system designed for very near facial fit and extremely effective airborne particle filtration. The classification 'N95' indicates that the respirator blocks at least 95% of very small test particles in thorough research.

Medical masks are often medical devices that use materials that block at least 95% of very small test particles, but they do not fit tightly to the face so that the user is not fully shielded. To have extra protection, they must be used in conjunction with other personal protective equipment (PPEs).

Following the recent epidemic, Santé Canada received valuable guidance to

improve the usage of masks and respirators. The Guidelines on coronavirus prevention from the Public Health Agency of Canada include guidance on wearing masks if needed and include:

If you are a good citizen, you cannot use a mask to avoid the spread of virus.

If you're not sick, wearing a mask will give you a false sense of comfort.

There is a possible possibility of contamination by misuse and reuse of masks.

They must also be updated regularly.

Nevertheless, if you have signs of virus as you are receiving or waiting for treatment, your health care provider may consider wearing a mask. Masks are a good part of infection prevention and control procedures in this case. The mask is a foil that serves to prevent tiny droplets from scattering as you toast or sneeze.

HOMEMADE FACE MASKS FOR 6 DIFFERENT SKIN CONDITIONS: RECIPES, BENEFITS, HOW TO USE

Do you experience acne issues, dry skin issues, scars, or age spots? Good skin isn't just the DNA. It also includes taking the right skincare regimen to cleanse, exfoliate, and moisturize the hair.

Some people attend spas to keep their appearance safe and young, but these trips can be costly over time. The effects are undeniable, but if, with a homemade face mask, you might

produce the same results?
Okay, you can, you can.
You should combine a DIY face mask with a variety of ingredients in your kitchen — such as avocados, oatmeal, tea, turmeric, or bananas.
From blemishes to dry skin, here are basic recipes for the treatment of common skin problems.

Acne mask

Acne in the United States is considered to be the most serious skin infection.
Titus occurs as pores clog blood, dead cells of the skin and bacteria, and acne contains red eyes, whiteheads, pimples, tumors and cysts.
However, the protein in egg whites can help destroy bacteria on the skin to avoid blemishes.
Ingredients:
2 to 3 egg whites Instructions:
Separate the yolk from the white egg and placed them in a tub.
Throw a cotton swab into the tub and coat the nose with the egg whites.

Enable the mask to rest 10-15 minutes.
Clean with a wet towel and apply a hydrating product.

Hyperpigmentation mask

Post-inflammatory hyperpigmentation is frequently the result of puberty, age, or sun exposure of darker skin regions.
Dermatological therapies may help reduce hyperpigmentation but are typically expensive.

You can save time by using a DIY turmeric mask and even decrease inflammation in your skin.
Ingredients:

Instructions:

1/2 tsp. turmeric powder 1 to 2 tbsp. raw honey

To make a paste, combine all ingredients in a pot.
Massage the paste softly across your nose.
Sit down and then clean with warm water for 10 minutes.

Clogged pores mask

Oatmeal and baking soda have exfoliating effects that can eliminate dead cells from the skin and obstruct pores.

Ingredients:

2 tsp. oatmeal
1 tsp. baking soda

Instructions:

In a mug, mix oatmeal and baking soda. Apply a few drops of water to create a paste gradually.
Massage the paste softly over your face and allow it to dry.
Wash and use a moisturizer in the spray.

Oily skin mask

Oily skin happens when you contain too much sebum in your pores, a normal skin oil.
Oils can block pores, cause acne and swelling.
Bananas can help absorb skin oil, while lemons help purify pores.

Ingredients:

1 banana
10 drops lemon juice
tsp. extra virgin olive oil

Instructions:

In a tub, mix the banana. To make a liquid paste, apply the lemon juice and olive oil.
Apply your face to the suit. Sit down for fifteen minutes, then wash with warm water.

Dry skin mask

A moisturizing face mask can help the skin retain moisture, relax, and itchy.

Ingredients:

half a cucumber
tbsp. aloe vera gel

Instructions:

Combine the cucumber and the aloe vera oil.
Massage the paste softly across your nose.

Let it sit and wash away with water for 30 minutes.

Wrinkles mask

Regular facial treatments can reduce the appearance of fine lines and wrinkles and improve the firmness of the skin.

Using avocado and cocoa powder to promote the development of collagen and sweeten skin with sugar.

Ingredients:

2 avocados
tbsp. raw honey
tbsp. cocoa powder

Instructions:

Mash the avocados in a cup and apply the paste of cocoa and sugar.
Massage the mask softly over your nose.
Let it lie down and scrub with warm water for 20 minutes.

How Do Face Masks Benefit The Skin?

A facial mask will refresh the skin and humidify it. These therapies are successful as the products will stay on the skin for about 10 to 30 minutes.

Nutrients and vitamins enter the flesh, purify the pores thoroughly and clear the outermost layer of dead tissue. Facial masks can purify, secure, exfoliate, smooth, and radiate the skin.

When you have no supplies (or time) to make a DIY mask, a rinse-off or peel-off over - the-count mask would still be better than a spa trip. A rinse-off mask is added as the mask dries with a warm or cold rag. Peel-off masks are gel-based for deep purification and exfoliation. You're going to add the mask, wait for it to harden, and then peel off.

The choice of a sheet mask is also available. You'll put a face sheet (containing nutrients and minerals) on your face instead of a cream or gel.

Facial masks do’s and don’ts
Here are a few do’s and don’ts to maximize the effectiveness of a facial mask.

DO'S:

Leave on the mask 10 to 30 minutes. This helps the skin to connect with ingredients. One option: Apply before entering the bath or shower.
Wash your face before applying a mask with water and a soft purifier. This makes the mask blend deeper into the face.

Upon cleaning the mask, add a moisturizer. Choose a face mask that is unique to your skin tone. Use an oil-free mask which does not obstruct pores whether you have oily or acne-prone skin.

Upon removing the mask, spray the cool water on your face to cover your pores.

DON'TS:

Should not use a mask if the skin or allergic reactions (rotting, burning, or rash) are present. Do not wear a mask every time. One weekend. Register only once or twice a week.

Don't keep the mask on for long, or you might get your skin irritated.

When drying the mask, don't clean your face. It can trigger redness and discomfort.

A daily skin care regimen can improve your complexion, counter acne, and manage your oiliness. Yet don't think you need a luxurious spa to produce better results.

You can make a homemade face mask and give your skin the food and hydration that it wants with ingredients in your kitchen.

MORE RECIPES

Forget to use your favorite spa time and energy. The key to big skin is too close to your oven! Enjoy these simple, handmade face mask recipes.

Make a Homemade Face Mask From Bananas
Everyone wants Botox because you've got bananas? That's right: you should use a banana to make your skin look and sound cleaner, as an all-natural home-made face mask. Mash in a smooth paste a medium-sized ripe banana and kindly apply it to your face and back. Set for 10 to 20 minutes and rinse off with cool water. A famous 1/4 cup of plain yogurt, 2 tablespoons of honey (a natural treatment for acne), and 1 medium banana are also available.

Eat a frozen "banana-sicle."
For your friends and family, peel and cut four ripe bananas half (in the middle) in the morning. Place a wooden ice cream stick on each piece's flat end. Place both of them on a sheet of wax paper and put them in a freezer. Serve them as simply yummy frozen banana-sicles a few hours away. If you want to do it, dip your frozen banana easily into six ounces of melting butterscotch or chocolate morsels (optional chopped nuts or shredded coconut), then refrigerate.

DIY Lemon Face Masks

Create a face to exfoliate and moisturize by combining 1 lemon juice with 1/4 cup of olive oil or sweet almond oil.

Milk Face Masks

Another place to find a luxurious spa at home is here. Mix 1/4 cup of powdered milk along with enough water to create a thick paste to make a homemade face mask. Coat the paste thoroughly, let it dry, then rinse with warm water. Your face is going to be new and rejuvenated!

How to Make a Homemade Face Mask with Oatmeal

If you want a quick pick-up that will make you feel better and look better, serve yourself facial oatmeal. Combine 1/2 cup of steam, not boiling, 1/3 cup of oatmeal. Once two to three Minutes of water and oatmeal have been resolved, mix 2 tablespoons of plain milk, 2 tablespoons of sweet wine, and 1 tiny egg white. Cover your face with a thin layer of mask and let it settle down for 10-

15 minutes. Rinse deeply with heated spray. (To prevent clogging the drain with granules, put a metal or plastic filter in your sink.)

Mayonnaise Face Masks

Would you spend money on pricey creams when you can use a home-made, calming face mask from your own refrigerator of whole-egg mayonnaise? Pour the mayonnaise over your face kindly and quit for about 20 minutes. Drain and shower with cold spray. Your skin should feel smooth and safe.

How to Make Yogurt Face Masks

You don't have to go to a spa to offer swift assistance to your skin. Slit a little yogurt on your face and let it stay for about 20 minutes to cleanse your skin and close your pores. Mix 1 teaspoon plain yogurt with 1/4 piece of orange juice, orange pulp, and 1 teaspoon aloe for a revitalizing face cream. Keep the water on your skin for five minutes or more before rinsing off.

Homemade Face Mask From Mustard

Place mild yellow mustard on your face to a bracing facial that calms and strengthens the skin. Try it first on a small training area to ensure that it would not irritate.

Make an Egg Face Mask

Go to the refrigerator for a little pampering and grab an egg. If the skin is dry and needs hydrating, remove the egg and beat the yolk. Fat skin takes the egg white and can be added to a lemon or honey. Using the entire egg for natural skin. Apply the egg, relax and wait for 30 minutes, and then rinse. You're going to enjoy your fresh new face.

CONCLUSION

It's not a new idea to make a DIY mask. Since Cleopatra's day, women have cooked their own skincare products, including soothing and calming masks.

At that moment, it was completely appropriate to take everything they wanted from the plants and flowers surrounding them. Today there is new interest in making your own face masks with a renewed interest in greening and protecting our planet and supplying ourselves with the safest and most effective skincare products.

Sadly, you can not avoid skin loss and can't stop the normal symptoms of aging. Your skin is exposed every day to various external hazards and may be harmed. Nothing takes a greater toll than time, of course. When we mature, our skin loses its elasticity and color, and shrinks, cracks, and hollows. Tools for skin care can help to fill and rejuvenate the skin. If you use a shop-purchased or a DIY face mask, you can stimulate healing and make your skin look healthier.

As is possibly well known, most commercially manufactured products contain a variety of additives, some of the natural and some of them synthetic. Although this may be accurate, no matter how careful these scientists are with their research, they may lose their effectiveness as the materials are refined to be included in the final product. And masks that are "completely natural" do not always contain the same skin levels that improve the natural substances that you can find in a DIY face mask.

While the use of shop-bought items from established brands can definitely be helpful, you know and trust that you must carefully tread. Know, you only have one skin and do whatever you can and protect it. With exposure to a variety of irritants as well as to unhealthy radiation, the skin will take a horrible beating daily.

It can all look dusty, ribbed, raw, scaly, or oily, and masks can be a perfect way to cope with this trauma. Before entering the costly market, however, you should try using a home-made face mask.

You can create a healthy and efficient DIY face mask with all the goodness of natural ingredients at half the cost and with very little effort. As long as you do your homework and look for the ingredients that best fit your face, you will make your own masks and uncover the natural secrets people have enjoyed for thousands of years.
It is an easy way to take care of the skin without putting toxins or toxic materials at risk. You stop

fried food, and you don't want to bring something that isn't healthy for you into your mouth, so why don't you treat your skin like this? When making your own masks, you can specifically regulate the mask you place on your face so that you know that only the finest nature can bring. This is genuine peace of mind, and an added effort to keep the skin young and healthy at any age is worth it.

www.ingramcontent.com/pod-product-compliance
Lightning Source LLC
LaVergne TN
LVHW052054160826
845678LV00015B/3226

* 9 7 9 8 4 7 5 6 7 1 7 4 0 *